1950s MODERN
BRITISH STYLE AND DESIGN

Susannah Walker

SHIRE PUBLICATIONS

Published in Great Britain in 2012 by Shire Publications
Ltd, Midland House, West Way, Botley, Oxford OX2 0PH,
United Kingdom.

44-02 23rd Street, Suite 219, Long Island City, NY 11101,
USA.

E-mail: shire@shirebooks.co.uk   www.shirebooks.co.uk

A CIP catalogue record for this book is available from the
British Library.

Shire Library no. 685.   ISBN-13: 978 0 74781 145 9

Susannah Walker has asserted her right under the
Copyright, Designs and Patents Act, 1988, to be identified
as the author of this book.

Designed by Tony Truscott Designs, Sussex, UK
and typeset in Perpetua and Gill Sans.

Printed in China through Worldprint Ltd.

12 13 14 15 16   10 9 8 7 6 5 4 3 2 1

COVER IMAGE
This 1955 room without a suite was just the kind of design
approved of by the Council of Industrial Design.

TITLE PAGE IMAGE
Small pieces of furniture like these were an easy way to
add a contemporary touch to a room.

CONTENTS PAGE IMAGE
Plans for a new city centre for Coventry were under way
well before the war was over.

IMAGE ACKNOWLEDGEMENTS
I would like to thank the people and institutions who have
allowed me to use illustrations, which are acknowledged as
follows:

Architectural Press Archive / RIBA Photographs
Collection, page 11; David Grant, pages 4, 40 (bottom);
Design Council Slide Collection at Manchester
Metropolitan university, pages 8, 34, 37 (top), 45
(bottom); Design Council / University of Brighton Design
Archives (photographer Leonard Taylor), pages 14, 17, 18,
19, 20, 21 (top), 25 (top); Geffrye Museum, page 41
(top); Getty Images, page 5; High Wycombe Furniture
Archive, pages 6, 34 (bottom), 42, 53 (bottom); Imperial
War Museum, pages 12, 13, 15; Liss Fine Art (copyright
Piper Estate), pages 24–5; Mirrorpix, page 32 (bottom);
N. Webster Collection, page 27 (top); Oliver Childs
(Homespunvintage.co.uk), page 54 (top);
Sheila Bownas (Flora-dora.co.uk), page 30.

All other images are from the author's own collection.

Shire Publications is supporting the Woodland Trust, the UK's leading woodland conservation charity, by funding the dedication of trees.

CONTENTS

INTRODUCTION

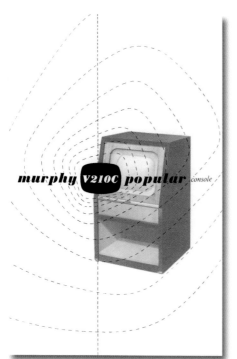

murphy V210C popular *console*

THE 1950s was the decade in which the British really embraced modern design for the first time, and it is easy to see why. After ten years of austerity and self-denial, caused first by the Second World War and then by the need to repay the massive debt that the country had accrued in fighting it, the time had come to look forward at last. There was an optimism in the air: a sense that this new, progressive Britain was going to be a better place for everyone. One important way this attitude was expressed was in a bright new style of design.

This was partly because objects themselves were part of the change, as higher living standards and improved technologies made household goods such as fridges, cookers and televisions available to the majority of people for the first time. But the new 'contemporary' style of design was also a direct reaction to the material deprivations of the war and post-war years.

It is hard now to imagine just how drab and run-down Britain looked in 1949, a shabby country full of patched-up bomb-sites, with empty shops and no new cars or buses to be seen. Cyril Connolly saw London in the 1940s as 'the largest, saddest and dirtiest of great cities, with its miles of unpainted, half-inhabited houses, its chopless chop-houses, its beerless pubs'.

What was true of the country as a whole was also the case in people's homes. Only a very few – newly weds and those with the misfortune to have been bombed out – had been able to buy furniture or crockery, and even these had been made to the plainest austerity designs. There were no ornaments or carpets to be had, no paint or wallpaper. Britain was inescapably dreary.

So when the last restrictions were lifted in the early 1950s, the urge to repair and redecorate must have been almost overwhelming. Along with this came a desire for something different. This was certainly a reaction to the war, but the move towards new colours and shapes had deeper roots as well. People genuinely did feel that Britain had changed since the war, and that their homes needed to reflect this.

London, like every city in the country, felt dirty, crumbling and old-fashioned at the start of the 1950s.

All of which meant that when the Festival of Britain opened its gates in 1951, its vision of a light and airy architecture and design was not only a welcome change from the London which surrounded it, but also a pointer to the new looks. This was exactly what its architects and designers had intended: the Festival style, with its friendly and organic

The Festival of Britain was intended as a tonic of colour, enthusiasm and good design.

By 1955, the 'Festival look' was part of the mainstream, in part due to companies like G Plan.

take on pre-war modernism, was a chance, according to director Gerald Barry, to 'represent the hopes in three-dimensional form of a better and brighter future'.

To a great extent, it worked. The kind of decoration and furnishings which permeated the Festival became the 'Contemporary Style'. Its hallmarks of pale wood, splayed legs to make furniture look lighter, the use of contrasting colours rather than brown or beige, the simple lines and open-plan living all typify how we think of the decade now.

But this was not the only way to be modern during the 1950s. Some artists and designers looked in a very different direction, trying to fashion the more romantic British tradition into a different version of the future. In many people's homes, the hunger for colour and pattern after austerity resulted in a riot of design across walls, plates and fabrics which had nothing to do with the simple functionalism of the Festival. As the decade went on, many people also looked to American goods and entertainments, seeing in their technicolour consumerist plenty a country where the future had already arrived and was being lived in.

This book will look at the many different ways in which the desire to be modern was expressed in the 1950s, from buildings and furniture to graphics and consumer goods, as well as the arguments that arose when these different ideas collided. Was the country becoming too Americanised and flashy in its new consumer paradise? Or were the designers of these new styles too detached from what it really meant to be British? It was certainly true that Great Britain wanted to turn itself into a modern nation after the war – but just how this was to be done was another question altogether.

New materials such as Formica and its British imitators brought colour into every part of the contemporary home.

A natural wood dining set with WARERITE tops by J. B. Heath Ltd.

DESIGN IS GOOD
FOR YOU

THERE is a tendency to see the Festival of Britain as a kind of 'big bang' from which the entire contemporary style burst, fully formed, into life: the only source of the bright colours, springy furniture and atomic patterning which dominated the decade from then on. Before 1951, we imagine a dun-coloured and tatty Britain of Victorian architecture and continuing rationing. The Festival marks the moment when the austerity of the post-war years ended, and the British people entered a future of consumer goods, plentiful food, contemporary furniture and teenagers; entered the 1950s in fact.

It is a potent myth, but like all good myths, it is a very simplified version of the real story. Not only had there been plenty of modern architecture and design before this moment, it had also been widely seen and promoted. Equally, the Festival itself contained much which did not fit this definition of the modern. The 8.5 million visitors also failed to undergo a Damascene conversion to the wonders of modern design on the spot; that process was much patchier and more disputed. Only by the end of the decade could the modern styles be said to have gone mainstream. And even then, the objects that the public chose did not always look as the designers of the Festival would have liked. The Festival of Britain, although important, was never quite as new or as influential as its promoters would like to claim.

Its designers knew full well that the Festival style was not born on 3 May 1951. One of the chief architects, Misha Black, admitted there was 'almost nothing on the South Bank which had not previously been illustrated in the architectural magazines'. Instead what arose on the South Bank was the distillation of developments in design and architecture which had been forming long before the war began.

Their genesis dated back more than twenty years, to the influential Stockholm Exhibition of 1930. This had as its manifesto: 'More beautiful things for everyday use'. 'Beautiful' in this context meant 'modern', and the whole exhibition was a showcase for high European modernism – the Paradise Restaurant was a three-storey box of glass and steel, while the room

Opposite:
Robin Day
designed this
'Music Lover's
Room' for the
Homes and
Gardens Pavilion
at the Festival
of Britain.

9

Abram Games' Festival logo symbolised the Festival's atmosphere of earnest gaiety.

The architecture might not have been all that innovative, but the South Bank was nevertheless very striking in 1951. One of the icons of the Festival, the Skylon (centre right) had no function other than to look futuristic and high-tech.

displays were unfussy and plain. But Stockholm's aim, 'to raise the taste and cultivation of our entire population', was a strong influence on the Festival. As important as the exhibition itself was the direction in which Swedish modernism developed afterwards. Designers increasingly worked with natural materials, such as brick and wood, along with organic shapes and a respect for craftsmanship to produce a less austere style which many in

Britain found easier to cope with. During the late 1930s, for British architects and designers this was how the future was going to be built.

The Second World War put these ambitions on hold, as Nissen huts and airfields took priority over anything as frivolous as style. But architects and designers did still have one arena in which to experiment, and this was exhibition design.

Throughout the war, the Ministry of Information produced a stream of exhibitions aimed at encouraging, exhorting and explaining every subject

The clean lines and open spaces of the 1930 Stockholm Exhibition were a key influence on the Festival of Britain.

The Army Exhibition of 1944 was a striking precursor of the Festival style. (Imperial War Museum TR 2427.)

from clothing coupons to the war in Japan. The Ministry's Exhibitions Department was where many of the Festival's designers, such as Misha Black and Cecil Cooke, worked during the war. Some of their creations were small-scale and portable, designed to tour the country to get their message across, while others were more striking showcases; what they all had in common was a noticeable modernism of design.

These were not the only places where the British might see modern design either. Posters instructed the public on everything from what to do in an air raid to how to eat, and many used the latest graphic style to get their message across. Among the most striking are Abram Games's posters for the Army, including his famous images of 'Your Britain, Fight for it Now'. These depict three of the most modern buildings from the late 1930s: Finsbury Health Centre, Impington Village College and Spa Green Flats. Combined with the Ministry of Information's exhibitions, which covered subjects like town planning and modern furniture as well as salvage and war, the subconscious message was clear. When a new Britain was built after the war, it would not only be better – it would also look very different.

This was not just a question of fashion. For the promoters of modernism – or, as they would have called it without a trace of embarrassment, 'good design' – their campaign had some of the qualities of a crusade. Furniture designer Robin Day remembered that design then was 'more a religion'. There was a real belief, shared with the originators of the Modern Movement and put into practice at events like the Stockholm Exhibition, that the right kind of architecture and products would change the lives of ordinary people for the better. In the case of architecture, this was a relatively straightforward premise: the indoor toilets, efficient kitchens and built-in heating of modern houses were a clear improvement on the slums they replaced. Better-designed products, like washing machines and fridges, would also make life easier. But beyond this lay an almost transcendental sense that 'good design' was morally improving too. People should like these new things because they would become better human beings as a result – and if necessary they would be made to like them.

One attempt to make this happen had already taken place during the Second World War in the form of the Utility scheme. Utility regulations set out detailed restrictions on the design of household goods (most notably clothes, furniture and pottery) in order to save raw materials and make the manufacturing process as efficient as possible. But just as food rationing was seen as having the additional benefit of improving the health of the nation,

Abram Games' posters specifically associated post-war reconstruction with modern architectural styles. (Imperial War Museum PST 2907.)

The simple lines of the Utility range were very different to pre-war furniture styles, and were unpopular with the public.

Utility pottery and furniture might also be a chance to reform popular taste. The furniture designer Gordon Russell, who was part of the committee overseeing Utility design, believed it was:

> Here is a chance to teach the public now growing up. To make them more critical of what is good design, what is bad and why, and so stimulate a much wider demand for better things.

Russell's Utility furniture, using light oak and simple shapes, was a mix of Scandinavian modernism and the indigenous British Arts and Crafts Movement. Ornament, mouldings and anything which might have used up extra wood or labour were gone, although a few curved edges and traditional influences were retained, keeping the results from being entirely angular and austere. Despite this, the furniture produced was still very different from the highly polished reproduction and Art Deco styles which had prevailed before the war. In contrast, Utility pottery was aggressively plain. Consisting of a range of simplified shapes glazed in white, it could easily have been the result of the heyday of the Bauhaus, and design critics loved it.

They were, however, the exception. Manufacturers hated what they saw as government interference in their business, while the public still preferred decoration. Most of the time this was an abstract debate because Utility wares were produced in such small quantities and nothing else was available. Even so, a black-market trade in carving decorations onto the furniture emerged, while the reaction against Utility pottery, which took the form of an almost insatiable demand for colour and pattern, will be seen later on. The much-hated pottery did end up having one lasting effect, in the design of a chunky teacup, decried at the time as 'elephantine' with 'clogs on for handles'. What the designers had invented, though, was the best-selling pottery shape ever: the mug.

There were more explicit attempts to influence people's taste too. The Council for Encouragement of Music and the Arts, a forerunner of the Arts Council, organised a number of exhibitions at the National Gallery on aspects of interiors and design during the war. These all illustrated the idea that the post-war world needed to be thought of as modern:

This wartime exhibition at the National Gallery encouraged people to think about their post-war homes in the most modern terms. (Imperial War Museum D 24947.)

> ... a simple beauty of form, enhanced by a sparing use of decoration, is the
> distinguishing feature of wares which could be produced at very moderate
> prices if a sufficiently large market were available for them ... good design
> costs little more than bad.

The end of the war did not mark the end of this attitude; indeed it did not
even mark the end of the Utility scheme. Consumers could buy only plain
white pottery until July 1952, and while a slightly larger range of
furniture was introduced in 1948, the last restrictions were lifted as late
as January 1953.

This continuation of wartime austerity was caused by financial pressures.
Britain desperately needed to revitalise its export industry in order to repay
its war debt, and to do this it needed to produce objects that other countries,
the USA in particular, would want to buy. Which in turn meant that good
design became not just a moral force but an important economic weapon
too. As early as 1944, Churchill's cabinet was debating the problem:

> Something like an industrial revolution has taken place in the United States
> over the last fifteen years – a revolution in Industrial Design. It has made our
> exports old-fashioned and less acceptable.

'Britain Can Make
It' was intended to
inspire the nation's
appreciation of
industrial design.

Britain would no longer be able to trade on tradition alone; that was the
clear message.

One result was the setting up that year of the Council of Industrial
Design (CoID), a body whose aim was 'the improvement of design in the
products of British Industry'. The CoID's manifesto
stressed that it was acting for the export interests of
the country in promoting 'Sales Appeal', but given the
subjective nature of its brief, it inevitably became
involved in the promotion of 'good design' too.

Both of these motives – the export drive and the
moral improvement – combined in the CoID's first big
post-war exhibition, 'Britain Can Make It'. Held at the
Victoria and Albert Museum in 1946, the aim was to
show how Britain was planning to beat swords into
ploughshares and 'take the lead in post-war markets'.
Despite the fact that the exhibition became known
as 'Britain Can't Have It' because most of the
exhibits were either prototypes or designed for
export only, it became an enormous popular success.
Over 1.5 million people queued along Exhibition
Road, and what they most wanted to know was not

People queued for hours to see the unobtainable consumer goods on display at the 'Britain Can Make It' exhibition.

how industrial design worked but what they might one day be able to buy for their homes. Thus the most popular section was the room sets, along with the displays of that rare luxury, patterned pottery, on Shop-Window Street.

On show was a gentle and fairly unthreatening version of modern design, which tended to follow the Utility designs in referencing traditional furniture shapes and fabrics, but even this was seen as scarily new. When the social

This was one of the more expensive kitchens on display in the exhibition.

research organisation Mass Observation surveyed visitors, they recorded comments such as 'I wouldn't buy it. It's not at all snug and cosy. It looks too much like an aircraft factory.' But the public was happy to look at anything, even if they didn't necessarily like it, as *Punch* magazine explained. 'Our eyes have become so accustomed to drab colour and austere cuts that we just haven't been able to resist this post-war opportunity to gaze into a brilliant shop window'.

There was one way in which the exhibition did expose its hordes of visitors to a very striking style of modern design, not so much in the exhibits as in the displays. Here was a real opportunity for young architects and designers to experiment, including a number who went on to work on the Festival of Britain, and they seized the chance with both hands.

Almost as soon as 'Britain Can Make It' had ended, the CoID (working alongside the shiny new Arts Council) was charged with creating the Festival of Britain. It comes as no surprise then that 'good design' was at the heart of the main exhibition on the South Bank. But the Council's

The Dome of Discovery and Skylon formed a deliberately futuristic architectural centrepiece for the Festival.

influence also meant that many of the displays bore a considerable resemblance to what had been shown in 1946, and were quite often designed by exactly the same people.

This then was the context in which the Festival of Britain was designed. A new style of modern architecture and interiors had been in the atmosphere for some time, even if it was not yet available to the public. Like a sort of visual roughage, people were meant to like it because it was good for you. But as we shall see, modern design was not always to everyone's taste.

When the gates opened in 1951, what shape did the brave new world of the Festival of Britain actually take? The most obvious answer – and the first impression gained by most visitors to the Festival – was the 'Dan Dare' landscape of the Dome of Discovery and the Skylon. But no one really expected to live in those, at least not straight away. In 1976 the art critic William Feaver gave this description of the more accessible elements of the South Bank:

> Braced legs, indoor plants, colour-rinse concrete, lily-of-the-valley splays of light bulbs, canework, aluminium lattices, Cotswold-type walling with picture windows, flying staircases, blond wood, the thorn, the spike, the molecule: all these became the Festival Style.

Such domestic design was at the heart of the Festival. Room sets for everything from a country parlour to a miner's kitchen could be seen in the Homes and Gardens Pavilion. These featured the newest furniture by designers such as Robin Day and Terence Conran, along with some more familiar Utility items as well. But interior design spilled out of the confines of the pavilion too: Ernest Race's innovative Antelope and Springbok chairs were scattered liberally over the public areas, and CoID had prepared the 'Design Index' – over 20,000 well-designed items specially selected for the Festival, all of which could be seen by visitors on a handy card index displayed under the arches at Charing Cross.

The modern home appeared elsewhere in the Festival, most obviously at the Exhibition of Architecture in Poplar, where a whole new neighbourhood was springing up in a soft Scandinavian mode of brick and flat roofs. Even the less likely setting of the Ulster Farm and Factory Exhibitions had as its

Weary festival-goers could rest their legs in Ernest Race's Springbok chairs, which could be found all over the site.

centrepiece a model farmhouse displaying the virtues of open-plan living and contemporary furniture.

One irony was that many of the new styles on display were born out of the same restrictions on materials which had produced the Utility designs. Terence Conran remembers that his furniture in the Homes and Gardens Pavilion was

> … mostly made out of welded reinforcing rod, which was about the only metal material you could get – you used to have to have a word with someone on a building site to buy some reinforcing rod as there was such an extraordinary shortage of materials in Britain at that time.

Other aspects of the contemporary were born from the same imperatives – thin legs, for example, used a lot less wood – while the architecture at Poplar was deliberately simplified to keep it affordable.

Much of what was on display nonetheless came from a very genuine desire to create a new style for the post-war world. The thin legs made furniture look less heavy; light woods brightened up a room without the need for ornamental carvings; room divider cupboards were designed to complement modern open-plan living; bright new fabrics brought colour into the home. And curved, cloud-shaped table tops were also a sign of living in a brand new world which did things differently.

Reactions to the styles on display varied enormously. The playwright Arnold Wesker went straight down to his local decorating shop in East London to buy the wallpaper designs he had just seen, only to be told, 'they wouldn't

The Festival Architecture Exhibition at Poplar showcased the reconstruction of a badly bombed East London neighbourhood.

This Festival room set showed glamorously non-Utility furniture by Ernest Race, Heals and other manufacturers.

sell down here', while a young architect renovating his own home on a budget found himself 'under the spell of strong primary colours ... used in strong, emphatic touches'. These influences did not always work as the original designers had intended. The Skylon produced imitators in the form of everything from standard lamps to pens, while the brightly coloured balls which had screened the Festival from the traffic of Waterloo Road would become decorative ends to coat-hooks, clocks and cruet sets for many years to come.

What the Festival did prove was that a good part of the British public was ready for a dose of modern design, especially if they were not forced to live in it. But the other reason why it was welcomed so thoroughly into people's hearts was that much of what was on show did not look very modern at all.

The design of the Festival did turn up in some fairly unexpected guises.

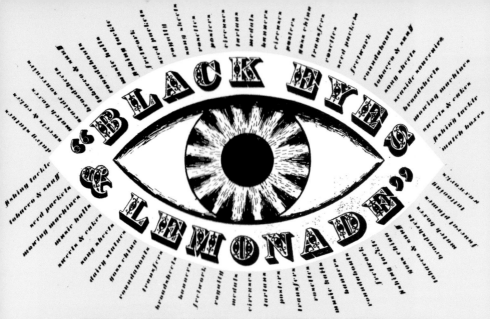

"BLACK EYES & LEMONADE"

A FESTIVAL OF BRITAIN EXHIBITION BY ARRANGEMENT WITH THE ARTS COUNCIL

BRITISH POPULAR ART

AND IN CONJUNCTION WITH THE SOCIETY FOR EDUCATION IN ART

WHITECHAPEL ART GALLERY

Barbara Jones

AUGUST 11th — 1951 — OCTOBER 6th

Daily 11-6 : Sundays 2-6 : Closed Mondays : Nearest Station Aldgate East

Shenval Press London and Hertford

DIFFERENT WAYS OF SEEING

DESPITE the best efforts of the CoID, not all of the Festival of Britain was decked out in its approved styles. At the start of the decade, artists and designers were also exploring other ways of being modern, many of which could be found at the Festival itself.

Right from the start, there had been a question mark over whether modern design was something which came naturally to the British at all. It was true that most of the modernism in Britain before 1950 was foreign in origin. The years leading up to the war had brought a number of émigré architects and designers to Britain as they fled from Fascism. The results were some of Britain's most modernist buildings, including the Highpoint flats and the De La Warr Pavilion in Bexhill. A similar influx had happened in print: foreign designers such as Lewitt-Him, Arnold Rothholz, Beverley Pick and Hans Schleger were widely used during the war when their British counterparts had been called up, bringing continental modernism to Post Offices and village halls right across the country.

For British people, the idea of being modern themselves was difficult. The painter Paul Nash out spelt this out as early as 1932:

> Whether it is possible to 'go modern' and still 'be British' is a question vexing quite a few people today ... The battle lines have been drawn up: internationalism versus an indigenous culture; renovation versus conservatism; the industrial versus the pastoral; the functional versus the futile.

Another painter and designer concerned with combining modernism and the British tradition was John Piper. He had embraced abstract painting in his paintings of the early 1930s, aligning himself with the European mainstream. By 1939 though, Piper had returned to the British landscape instead, choosing representational subjects such as historic churches and country houses. His neo-Romanticism was not intended to be reactionary; instead it was an attempt to find a new visual language which also incorporated British

Opposite:
The 'Black Eyes and Lemonade' exhibition: a very different approach to good taste.

During and after the war, émigré designers like Dorrit Dekk brought a very different graphic style to Britain.

John Piper's mural of 'The Englishman's Home' from the exterior of the Homes and Gardens Pavilion.

tradition. These debates were played out right in the heart of the Festival of Britain, where Piper's mural, 'The Englishman's Home', stretched for 50 feet along the back of the Homes and Gardens Pavilion. Although modern in style, it portrayed no contemporary architecture at all.

Such arguments posed an additional challenge for the Festival of Britain design team, whose overall brief had been to illustrate 'the British contribution to civilisation, past, present and future'. On top of this tricky balancing act between the British and the modern, they had to incorporate history, as the exhibition needed to celebrate the Great Exhibition of 1851 – a similarly great national event, but one whose curlicues and excesses sat in direct opposition to the contemporary style.

The Lion and the Unicorn were used to represent the serious and eccentric sides of the British character.

Parts of this were managed quite easily. A small model of the 1851 Great Exhibition site sat at the foot of the Shot Tower, looking slightly like the afterthought it was. Another late addition to the festival was the Lion and the Unicorn Pavilion, which aimed to describe that very nebulous concept, the British character, and thus included everything from Shakespeare and a Constable painting to a plaster model of Lewis Carroll's White Knight. The tensions here led to an interesting mix of styles, as eighteenth-century script hung from the technologically advanced lamella roof pavilion. Similar problems faced the Land of Britain display (whose subject was never going to lend itself to a modern treatment) where F. H. K. Henrion created a great white oak, which was more of a surrealist fantasy than anything futuristic.

The Festival Pleasure Gardens were intended as light relief from the more serious South Bank.

Away from the South Bank, other sites favoured the British over the contemporary. The 37 acres of the Festival Pleasure Gardens at Battersea were almost entirely devoted to the twin national characteristics of whimsy and humour, and the best-remembered feature there encapsulated this. Rowland Emmett's Far Tottering and Oyster Creek Railway was a monument to British eccentricity, illogicality and charm. Flamboyantly over-specified with

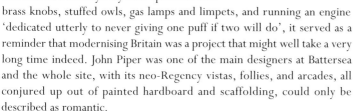

The Far Tottering and Oyster Creek Railway brought Rowland Emmett's drawings into shaky life at Battersea.

brass knobs, stuffed owls, gas lamps and limpets, and running an engine 'dedicated utterly to never giving one puff if two will do', it served as a reminder that modernising Britain was a project that might well take a very long time indeed. John Piper was one of the main designers at Battersea and the whole site, with its neo-Regency vistas, follies, and arcades, all conjured up out of painted hardboard and scaffolding, could only be described as romantic.

A similarly ornate anti-modernism could be found in other parts of the Festival too, most notably the Whitechapel Art Gallery's contribution, 'Black Eyes and Lemonade'. A celebration of the popular arts, curated by Barbara Jones and Tom Ingram, the exhibition contained everything from ornate Victorian pub mirrors to a modern fireplace in the shape of an Airedale terrier. This championing of popular taste was not only advanced for the time, it was also an implied rebuke to the improving approach of the South Bank.

One of the most influential aspects of the Festival was also historic in origin, and that was its typography. The approved typefaces were based on an early nineteenth-century display type known as Egyptian. Once again, this was less a startling innovation on the part of the Festival than a reflection of existing trends, but the result was that similar styles were being used on everything from packaging to buildings right up to the early 1960s.

Designers could choose between a range of Festival typefaces in order to 'avoid monotony'.

Regency-inspired patterns like these wallpaper designs were popular throughout the decade.

Outside the Festival and its gung-ho futurism, a genuine ambivalence about modernism could also be found. While most people were undoubtedly looking forward to the modern world of the Welfare State, Mr Therm and technicolour living, some were also worried by the changes. There was a fear that traditional British virtues and styles would disappear for ever. In design, one result of this was a Regency revival, which attempted to create a contemporary take on an historical style. This was in part a result of necessity, particularly in the early years of the decade when modern furniture was hard to find and expensive when it could be tracked down. Many magazines and interior designers showed rooms that mixed a selection of old and new furniture, because this was the way their readers would be living. But many of those readers were not yet ready to live in a very modern home either.

The tension between the modern and the historic permeated some surprising aspects of British life. In the later years of the decade it could also be seen on the streets, as working-class teenagers opted to be either an Edwardian-styled Teddy Boy or a clean-lined Mod. So by the early years of the 1960s, the battle between traditional and modern influences was quite literally being fought out on England's seafronts.

Lewitt-Him's illustrations for Kia-Ora were typical of his whimsical approach.

The desire to combine these two impulses in a uniquely British version of the modern, inspired by painters like John Piper, continued to be important too. Piper himself created several designs for wallpapers and fabric, and even furniture, all of which were popular throughout the decade; for their buyers, these designs would have represented the modern as surely as the contemporary styles.

Many other designers were inspired by this neo-Romantic approach, and the results could be seen on book covers, posters and illustrations as well as on the walls and curtains of people's homes.

The lighter, more frivolous attitude of Piper's Battersea Gardens did not evaporate after the Festival either. The British tradition of whimsy continued strongly, with illustrators such as Bruce Angrave and Lewitt-Him creating popular advertising campaigns and illustrations. Even more modern designers like Tom Eckersley produced figures which tended to smile cheerfully, something he explained with hindsight: 'Nearly all my solutions had a whimsical, humorous side. I think that this was something to do with the climate after the hostilities ceased.' This sense of release and cheerfulness after the war must have been felt by much of the population, and the resulting mood often lightened the contemporary style.

By the later years of the 1950s it might have seemed that modern design was, if not triumphant, then certainly in the ascendant. But the tensions between 'Britishness' and modernity were never fully resolved, and they once again revealed themselves in the form of an international exhibition. At the Brussels Expo in 1958, the British Pavilion had a strikingly modern exterior but was filled with an interior display of British whimsy which would not have looked out of place in the Lion and Unicorn Pavilion. The brochure drawings, by Barbara Jones, the curator of 'Black Eyes and Lemonade', also oscillate between high-tech chemical plants and a more cuddly national vision of 'Scottie' dogs and friendly policemen. Throughout the 1950s, Britain could never imagine itself as wholly modern, no matter how hard the nation tried.

A cheery optimism pervaded the graphics of the era, as in this travel poster by Tom Eckersley.

Barbara Jones's illustrations for the Brussels Expo depict traditional British imagery but in a modern style.

A MODERN COUNTRY

IF ASKED, the British people would almost certainly have felt that they were living in a new and exciting age during the 1950s. Modern styles were everywhere by the middle years of the decade, even if they did not always conform to the blueprint laid down in 1951.

In part this was again down to the expense of reconstruction. Large numbers of buildings were being built, houses and flats in particular, but the need for speed and economy meant that they were mass-produced and kept simple. In the end, the low-rise brick of the Festival of Britain Building Exhibition at Poplar was a better forecast of the new urban landscape than the exuberant architecture of the South Bank. Almost every new building was commissioned by governments and local authorities, with private licences almost impossible to procure, so the scope for innovation or experiment was negligible. Individual buildings such as schools and shopping centres allowed architects a little bit more leeway, and in a few cases such as Harlow and Coventry, city centres were intended as showpieces of reconstruction, but even here flamboyance was not encouraged.

The modern houses in the New Towns and elsewhere were nonetheless very different, not only in the quality of their kitchens and bathrooms, but also their smaller rooms and open-plan design. In the long run this would change how people furnished their rooms. At first, though, their recently arrived occupants just carried on as normal; as one disapproving visitor to Harlow discovered, 'The rooms certainly struck one as small, perhaps because they were stuffed with unsuitable furniture. Oversized suites and clumsy sideboards hit the eye.'

The Festival style did produce a couple of fully realised buildings. On the South Bank, the Royal Festival Hall had always been intended to be permanent, while outside London the notable exception to austerity architecture was Coventry Cathedral. Commissioned in 1951, although not completed until 1962, it is often described as the fullest architectural development of the ideas of the early 1950s, in its combination of the modern structure with works by artists such as John Piper and Graham Sutherland.

Opposite:
Bright fabrics
like this design
by Sheila Bownas
provided an easy
way to bring
colour into
the home.

This did not mean that modern architecture was absent from most people's lives. Once more, exhibition design came to the rescue, allowing architects and designers to develop adventurous ideas and styles in a temporary form. While many of these were for trade shows such as the British Industries Fair, public exhibitions such as the Radio Show and Ideal Home Show introduced many more people to striking architectural ideas than would ever have seen a new building.

Designed by Misha Black, this stand for *Farmers' Weekly* is the Festival style in microcosm.

Despite the restrictions, modern design could still be seen all over the streets of Britain's towns and cities. The first five years of the decade were the

With its vast Graham Sutherland tapestry set in Basil Spence's building, Coventry Cathedral was the lasting monument of the Festival style.

heyday of the advertising poster. Before the advent of commercial television in 1955, this was still the most prestigious way for a company to advertise. Large billboards were ubiquitous, concealing drabness and dereliction with a splash of fresh new graphic design. Many designers had made their name during the war, including Tom Eckersley, Abram Games and Lewitt-Him, along with a new generation including Patrick Tilley and Harry Stevens, but British companies were also employing some

of the great continental names such as Donald Brun, Raymond Savignac and Jean Colin. Not every poster was a masterpiece, of course, but they were all colourful.

A continued belief in the improving powers of good design meant that these designers were also used by the government and its newly nationalised industries, so modern graphic design was brought to the broadest possible audience, whether they were waiting in the queue at the post office or thinking about travelling by train.

Within people's homes the contemporary style was beginning to take hold, but perhaps not in the way in which its early prophets had intended. Modern furniture was at least being produced: designers such as Robin Day, Ernest Race and a young Terence Conran were creating new ranges of lightweight furniture to suit smaller homes and new times. Features such as metal legs and plywood frames, which began as a result of austerity, were now fashionable rather than necessary.

These furnishings were available to only a very small minority of people, not just because they were expensive – which they were – but also because

Terence Conran set up his own company in the 1950s in order to produce modern furniture.

they were hard to find. A very few shops in London, such as Heals and Woollams, stocked the style, and outside London, those who wanted to furnish their home in a contemporary way found it very difficult indeed.

Only a small number of companies opted to manufacture the new style, the best known being Hille, Kandya and Ernest Race's own company, Race Furniture. Because of both the conservatism of the public and to

Frank Guille's designs for Kandya were some of the most adventurous available in the early years of the decade.

an even greater extent the resistance of retailers, they found it hard to sell their designs, and both Hille and Race Furniture soon ended up concentrating on the more lucrative and forward-thinking contract furnishings market.

There were a couple of exceptions to this. One was the High Wycombe firm of Ercol, whose lighter interpretation of a Windsor chair had originally been produced as an inexpensive Utility design in 1944. The design was much-beloved of the CoID, but it also sold well for many years after the restrictions had been lifted. The real success story of in modern furnishings, however, was G Plan, which went into production in 1953 just as the Utility restrictions ended. The designs were undoubtedly modern, featuring many contemporary ideas such as room dividers, mix-and-match pieces and Scandinavian-inspired shapes. But what made it a real success was the marketing. G Plan advertised directly to the consumer in magazines rather than relying on retailers for promotion – a rarity then. More importantly though, ranges were kept in production for many years, so consumers could add to their rooms when they felt able to afford it rather than having to buy a whole suite at once.

G Plan furniture was the first modern furniture brand to break through into the popular market.

Even G Plan had just a small share of the overall furniture market, which was still dominated either by reproduction designs, or by the boxy, highly polished furnishings which had been popular before the war. Part of the reason for this – and a big problem for the evangelical prophets of modern design – was that many manufacturers simply did not see the need to update their products. The public had been starved of new goods for so long that they would, frankly, buy almost anything. The *Architectural Review* had predicted this as early as 'Britain Can Make It':

> The CoID has had the unenviable task of selling *design* to manufacturers who must know only too well that *output*, however shoddy, cannot possibly overtake demand for several years to come.

This situation continued for a surprisingly long time; it has been estimated that the supply of furniture finally caught up with the demand in the very last years of the 1950s.

Lazy manufacturers and insatiable consumer demand were only part of the story. As we will see in the next chapter, there was also a widespread resistance to contemporary furniture and what it represented. This did not mean that people wanted nothing new in their houses; rather that it felt too daring, and potentially too extravagant, to buy big pieces of modern design. Just as colourful advertisements brightened up the outdoor streetscape while

Not everything in the home could be modernised – only one in twenty households had central heating by 1960.

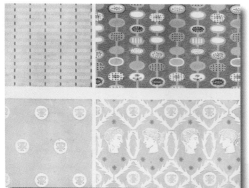

contemporary buildings were thin on the ground, householders also went for cheaper and less permanent ways of modernising their homes. What they bought instead of the chairs and sideboards was a whole range of smaller items, from crockery to wire fruit bowls, newspaper racks to vases, which brought in modern style at an affordable price. Also popular, for the same reasons,

Above: These wallpaper patterns came in pairs, with the bolder design intended for a feature wall.

grafton furnishing fabrics

Grafton Homecraft

A new all-cotton texture fabric, specially created to enhance the charm of the latest ideas in modern design and colour. 48" wide at about 9/11d per yard.

...in exciting contemporary designs. Grafton furnishing fabrics are obtainable from all good furnishing shops and stores, or write for name of nearest stockists to:

F. W. GRAFTON & CO. LTD., FURNISHING DEPARTMENT, 65 OXFORD STREET, MANCHESTER 1.

Right: Boldly patterned fabrics like these were soon available to suit every budget.

were smaller pieces of furniture, hence the ubiquity of the small, kidney-shaped coffee table or splay-legged telephone stand in the hall.

They also took to one of the key aspects of the contemporary style: its bright new palette. Colour was one of the most persistent memories of the Festival of Britain and also one of the easiest ways to banish the dreariness of war and austerity, as one designer remembered: 'The days of varnish, brown paint and porridge wallpaper were served notice in 1951. We were no longer afraid to start with white and then use any colour or combination from the rainbow. It was great fun.'

The trend caught on because colour was cheap too. New chemicals meant that easy-to-use paints were available in a wider and brighter range, allowing householders to add a splash of colour to their houses at very little cost (or two or three colours). One very contemporary statement was the 'feature wall', where a single wall was either wallpapered or painted a contrasting, and often very deep, shade. While fashions in colour did change over the decade, getting first deeper and then moving to a more natural range of shades, the use of contrast was a constant throughout.

These new colours could be brought into the home in other inexpensive ways too. Gaily patterned furnishing fabrics were a very popular choice throughout the decade. As with the furnishing firms, the best designers of the time, like Lucienne Day, Jacqueline Groag and Marianne Mahler, found themselves selling to a small clientele through exclusive shops like Heals. The difference was that the colours and styles did percolate down the market, as their works inspired – or were entirely ripped off by – cheaper copies.

China and tableware also worked in a similar way, allowing consumers to bring a touch of the contemporary into their homes without breaking the bank or frightening the in-laws. After ten years of plain white pottery, consumers reacted by demanding bright colour and pattern on everything. Soon forward-thinking manufacturers like Midwinters and J&G Meakin were producing modern shapes too, inspired by designs that had been evolving in America during the war.

It is worth remembering that even in industries like these where there was a demand for the modern, it was by no means the whole of the market. Fabric companies were still weaving Regency stripes and delicate florals as well as abstract designs, while the pottery firms of Stoke sold many traditional sprigged and Chinese blue patterns on traditional shapes alongside their contemporary offerings. For every company like Midwinter or Edinburgh Weavers who were committed to the new style, there were ten who did just fine producing the same traditional

Bright colours and all-over patterns characterised contemporary tableware, like this set by J&G Meakin.

you set it...
and forget it!

BENDIX

automatically gives you . . .

the time of your life!

BENDIX
Gives you workless washdays at the touch of a dial—it doesn't just assist you or merely do some of the hard work . . . BENDIX does the whole job . . . *automatically*

SOAKS · WASHES · RINSES THREE TIMES
DAMP DRIES CLOTHES · DRAINS & SWITCHES OFF *all by itself*

Write for full particulars to: DEPT. K
BENDIX HOME APPLIANCES LTD. ALBION WORKS · KINGSBURY ROAD · BIRMINGHAM 24

The new labour-saving devices were sold on the promise of a carefree life for the housewife.

Opposite:
A modern fitted kitchen made just the same promises of leisure and freedom.

designs they had done before the war. As with the market for furniture, there was so much pent-up demand that consumers would, for a long time, buy almost anything that their factories could produce.

This did not mean that the British people had rejected the grand vision of modernism: more that they found it first in different places. And perhaps the most important of these was the kitchen. Before the war, the Modern Movement had seen the kitchen as a place where rational design really could create 'a machine for living in'. For once, the public had agreed with the designers. At 'Britain Can Make It', the kitchen displays had been amongst the most popular features in the exhibition, while a survey in the same year showed that the one piece of furniture that housewives most wanted was a kitchen cabinet.

But the modern kitchen was not just about clean lines and fitted units: both 'Britain Can Make It' and the Festival of Britain had also displayed the very latest labour-saving devices such as refrigerators and washing machines – the real reasons why the kitchen became the centre of modernity in the home.

Before the war such luxuries had been the preserve of only the most privileged households, but as wages rose, prices dropped and hire purchase controls were relaxed, they became more and more affordable for the average household. They were also becoming more necessary too. War had pretty much put an end to domestic service, and it has been suggested that in the years after 1945, the middle-class housewife worked harder and longer than she ever had before. No wonder then that when devices like the washing machine, the electric cooker and the refrigerator (which put an end to the need for almost daily shopping trips) arrived, they were welcomed with open arms. Even at the end of the decade, they were by no means universal: as late

Living begins with **LEISURE...**

LEISURE MADE

Test it ... Try it ...

SINKS and KITCHEN CABINETS

Leisure Sinks in lustrous coloured enamel or stainless steel.

Wide range of standard kitchen cabinets in a choice of colours.

Adds real spaciousness to the smallest kitchen.

Our Kitchen Planning Department will help you to plan a 'Leisure' kitchen.

Write for full details — today!

Everybody Likes Leisure

SPECIALISTS IN KITCHEN EQUIPMENT SINCE 1936

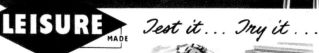

Easy running Drawer with Cutlery partition

Vegetable Basket Racks

Specially fitted Broom Cupboard

Bucket Filler Mixing Tap under Sink

Crockery drying Cabinet

Sink Tidy Basket inside door

Household accessories became colourful fashion items, right down to the humble toilet brush.

IF YOU DON'T KNOW WHAT THIS IS
...your guests certainly won't know either!

All you see of this lavatory set by Addis, the brush people, is a gay-coloured polythene bell. The brush sits pretty, hidden inside. Nylon tufted, it can't rot or go sogey—and won't drip either! Nylon being non-absorbent, a shake as it leaves the bowl rids the brush of moisture.

And it's so hygienic. The open back of the bell allows the air to circulate round the brush, keeping it dry and fresh.

Choose your Addis Lavatory Set in red, green, blue, yellow, black or white. The brush is standard, with a white plastic handle and black tufts. The set costs 10s complete.

MAKE SURE IT'S AN ADDIS! There are lots more efficient, colourful Addis brushes. See them at your hardware shop or store.

Addis
Addis Limited, Brush-works, Hertford

This 1950s model of television was the cheapest that Murphy produced after the war, but at £66 it was still very expensive.

murphy V150

as 1960, only 5 per cent of households in Wales owned a fridge.

More affordable was the fitted kitchen, intended to be hygienic and labour saving. Although the top-of-the-range kitchens were expensive, there was plenty of scope for DIY to create the effect without the cost. A manufactured kitchen was more expensive but had two main selling points, reflected in brand names like 'Leisure' and 'Californian': it saved time for the harassed modern housewife, and it was American-style – which had to be good.

This modern kitchen was not only efficient, it was also very colourful. Now servant-less, the suburban housewife could expect to spend a lot more time there than she ever had before, so the kitchen became a cheerful and attractive place for the first time. New technologies helped, as materials like Formica and its imitators brought colour and pattern onto worktops and kitchen tables which had previously been plain wood. Decoration and colour also spread to articles which had conventionally been dull and utilitarian, like storage jars and saucepans. Even dustpans and buckets became bright, thanks to the development of new kinds of plastics.

Outside the kitchen, the single piece of technology which most represented the future was the television. The rise of the TV was extraordinarily fast, and by 1956, 48 per cent of households had one, something which would have been unimaginable in 1951. Ironically, the television set itself took a long time to look modern – for the first half of the decade at least they tended to look like nothing so much as a 1930s radiogram with an out-dated veneer finish. This was partly because it took much longer to redesign a complex piece of machinery and retool the machines to make it. More importantly though, manufacturers did not need to rely on design as a selling point because once again supply could not keep up with demand. But it was also true that televisions were inherently modern, and so could wear whatever they liked.

The television also became an easy-to-read symbol for the modern: Guinness advertisements sprouted television aerials, and a television is among the many items from the ultra-contemporary home depicted on the Homemaker plates sold by Woolworths. The idea of a television could also be used to update products which were not themselves any different. For example, furniture manufacturers advertised 'Telepouffes', which were very much like an ordinary pouffe only with contemporary legs and a modern name. Similarly, pottery firms produced 'television sets', which were cups with extended saucers to hold biscuits and sandwiches, ideal for sitting down to watch the latest programmes. But these designs were nothing new: before the war they had been sold as 'croquet sets'. Television made them modern once again.

A television was just one of the modern icons pictured on Woolworths' Homemaker crockery.

By the end of the 1950s, the homes of Britain were very different places, and in ways in which the pioneers of the Festival of Britain would, perhaps, have approved of. There were probably few houses left which did not contain a small nod to the contemporary world, even if that was only a bright storage tin, a single wallpapered wall or a television. But this conversion was not a straightforward process, and the complaints and arguments about the way in which homes were changing were as many and varied as the designs themselves.

HYDRANGEA BLUE

TURQUOISE

PINE GREEN

TUFTED LARCH

OAK APPLE FAWN

BERRY RED

WILD RHODIE

EARTH BROWN

A characteristic range of 1950s colours from the early part of the decade.

NOT OVER HERE

Britain might have been embracing the modern, but this did not mean that everyone agreed on what the word meant. Throughout the decade, there were a number of different interpretations available, and at a time when designers believed in their work with an almost evangelical fervour, this led to arguments.

The most obvious point of conflict was over contemporary design itself. High-end designers felt that their work had been copied and debased by the high street, as Robin Day recollected:

> Much popular furniture grew thin metal legs with balls at the end, in ill-considered emulation of Ernest Race's chairs for the Festival of Britain … tables boasted amorphous 'organic' shapes in debased versions of the Cloud Table by Neil Morris.

This was not just an argument about the quality of workmanship. For designers like Day, the very nature of their modern design with its emphasis on fitness for purpose had been radically misunderstood. They believed that the style was being applied as a superficial veneer by manufacturers who had failed to grasp the purpose behind it, as Stephen Spender complained in 1959: 'The aim seems to be to look functional rather, perhaps, than to be it. The concept of function translates itself into bareness, simplicity, squareness or roundness, solidity, seriousness.'

The manufacturers could have replied that the designers had also failed to translate the ideas of the Modern Movement into action. Rather than supplying good design for all, they were producing it only for a very elite few. The furniture of Day and Race was beyond the means of all but the most affluent consumers, leaving everyone else with no choice but to buy the 'debased' versions on their local high street.

There was nonetheless some truth in the accusation that much of what was being sold as 'contemporary design' had very little to do with its original inspiration. Colour, pattern and novelty were the key features, and in most

Opposite:
By the mid-1950s even bedroom furniture was becoming contemporary, as this G-Plan brochure shows.

cases had little to do with fitness for purpose – unless that purpose was a cheery fashionability. The pottery of the 1950s provides an excellent example, apparently designed in opposition to every ideal of the Modern Movement. Plates were squared off rather than round, and so were more difficult to produce, while hand-painted patterns went across the plate rather than round the rim – again, a much less efficient process. On top of that, the main criterion for choosing a pattern seemed to be that it had never been used on pottery before. Formica, textiles and graphics were used as inspiration, while pictorial subjects ranged from pot plants and furnishings to French street scenes – all of which were peculiar things to put your food on if you thought about it for too long. But they looked modern, and that was the only thing that mattered.

Because contemporary design was expensive to buy, it inevitably got mixed up with the British class system too. In 1953, the Design and Industries Association, which had been promoting the cause of modernism and fitness for purpose since 1915, set up an exhibition called 'Register Your Choice' at Charing Cross Station. Once again, this was intended as a

By the middle of the 1950s, the contemporary style was widely available on the high street.

demonstration of how 'good design' was simply better. The display contrasted two living rooms, one furnished with 'old-fashioned' furniture, the other fitted out in the latest contemporary equivalents. The comparison was, to say the least, loaded, because the traditional room had been overstuffed with some spectacularly ugly furniture.

Despite their best efforts, the DIA did not quite get the results they wanted. The rooms were almost equally popular, but unskilled and semi-skilled working-class visitors strongly favoured the traditional sitting room over the contemporary version. A young typist admitted that she loved the modern room, but nonetheless summed up the invisible obstacles that stood in the way of the style's acceptance:

> I would never live in it. For one thing, my family would have a fit, they'd think I'd gone quite mad and all arty. You see, I'd have to be a different person, I'd have to read the best books and listen to the Third Programme, don't you agree?

There were other problems with the officially sanctioned version of 'contemporary' too. One was the question of the three-piece suite. The CoID did not like suites, because they wasted space in the smaller houses that were being built, had to be bought all at once and could not be adapted. In short, they were not 'good design'. As a result, the Council never showed suites in exhibitions, and they had not

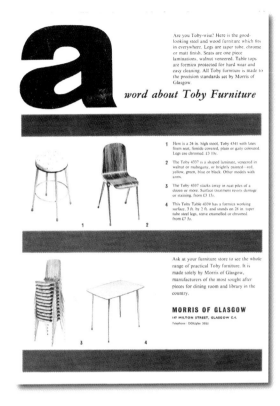

a *word about Toby Furniture*

Are you Toby-wise? Here is the good-looking steel and wood furniture which fits in everywhere. Legs are taper tube, chrome or matt finish. Seats are one piece laminations, walnut veneered. Table tops are formica protected for hard wear and easy cleaning. All Toby furniture is made to the precision standards set by Morris of Glasgow.

1 Here is a 24 in. high stool, Toby 4341 with latex foam seat, fionide covered, plain or gaily coloured. Legs are chromed. £3 19s.

2 The Toby 4337 is a shaped laminate, veneered in walnut or mahogany, or brightly painted—red, yellow, green, blue or black. Other models with arms.

3 The Toby 4337 stacks away in neat piles of a dozen or more. Surface treatment resists damage or staining. from £3 13s.

4 This Toby Table 4339 has a formica working surface. 3 ft. by 2 ft. and stands on 28 in. taper tube steel legs, stove enamelled or chromed from £7 5s.

Ask at your furniture store to see the whole range of practical Toby furniture. It is made solely by Morris of Glasgow, manufacturers of the most sought after pieces for dining room and library in the country.

MORRIS OF GLASGOW
147 MILTON STREET, GLASGOW C.4.
Telephone: DOUglas 3922

Morris and Co. of Glasgow were among the few high-end stores outside London. They also manufactured their own modern designs.

This 1955 pattern, 'Old MacDonald's Farm', must have been quite a distraction from the food itself.

The first room in 'Register Your Choice' was meant to appear overstuffed and old-fashioned.

been available under the Utility regulations either. But people, real people, did want a proper three-piece suite, believing that it looked homely and more comfortable. They also believed that these styles provided better defence against draughts, something which was probably true.

Other subconscious reasons must have played a part in these choices too. Buying a three-piece suite was almost as important a part of setting up home after marriage as buying a bed; to buy single chairs suggested a lack of seriousness or commitment. For some people, this perceived lack of respectability was a problem with all modern design. Mass Observation interviewed a married woman visitor to 'Register Your Choice' who felt that the contemporary room was 'very much for a rather immoral type of person – well it's out to impress, it's not sincere', while another man thought that only the traditional design could give children the right idea. What that idea was, he did not say.

The sense still lingered that modern design would never be entirely British. For example, complaints were made against the contemporary 'coupe' shape of pottery – designed without a rim – because this left nowhere for a proper Englishman to put his mustard.

There was always one easy way to criticise something for being un-British, and that was to call it American. In the case of the pottery, this happened to be true, as the new mustard-impeding shapes had been directly inspired by American post-war designs, but the term could be extended to almost anything that was 'different'. America was the land of plenty, novelty and excess, the place where the future that Britain could only dream about had already arrived. This meant, of course, that complaining about 'Americanisation' became an easy shortcut for those who did not like the changes taking place in Britain during the 1950s. Americanisation quickly came to stand for a whole list of perceived problems, from Teddy Boys and television to consumer goods and advertising, as well as bigger issues such as the decline of a traditional working-class culture and even the loss of British status on the world stage.

For designers, Americanisation meant two things: obsolescence and streamlining. Planned obsolescence – the idea that objects like cars or washing machines were being produced not to ideas of function or good working order but for disposability and fashion – was an affront to

The contemporary room displayed in 'Register Your Choice' did not prove as appealing as the organisers had hoped.

It could mean A HOLD UP

MAKE *YOUR* CALLS AS BRIEF AS POSSIBLE

GPO

Not even the British GPO could resist the glamour of American imagery sometimes.

every tenet of modernism that designers and architects had believed in. This was irresponsible design, perhaps even immoral.

Streamlining also challenged British notions of 'good design' head on. The name and forms originated with car design in the 1930s, where the shapes could be justified, almost, as a functional response to the needs of speed. But in America, the styling spread to almost every kind of consumer product imaginable. By the time that Britain caught up in the mid-1950s, American cars were a baroque confection of fins, chrome and detailing, and the look had spread to everything from fridges to diners. British designers hated the excess and superficiality of the style, but articulated their dislike by complaining these things did not move and so aerodynamics had no place in their design whatsoever. These two factors together came to represent everything which was wrong with popular taste: a 'gross and flamboyant' vulgarity which was just not British.

Americanisation worked in more subtle ways as well, and one example of this was the way in which food was pictured throughout the decade. This was the area where the deprivations of the war had been most deeply felt, and for longest, as the last food rationing only ended in 1954. So the ideas of restraint and minimalism were never going to be popular here. Instead, the visual language was taken from American advertising: saturated technicolour photography and hyper-realist drawings dominated. But above all, there was always more than enough food. In photographs, a dish was never shown alone but always surrounded by others, while advertisements dripped with a cornucopia of fruit, sweets and puddings.

British people wanted this American land of plenty in whatever form they could have it. The popularity of everything from advertising to rock and roll, leisure kitchens to milk bars, was clear for all to see. For British designers though, this was a blow. It meant that the modernist project, as represented by Utility design and the Festival of Britain, had failed. They had envisaged their own gently modernist taste trickling down the social scale until everyone had been morally improved by the design of their furniture. In fact the exact opposite had happened. A popular culture of Teddy boys and

Opposite: Almost any product might be sold by associating it with America.

Silhouette American Bras

THE FIGURE SECRET OF AMERICAN WOMEN — IN BRITAIN FOR THE FIRST TIME

SMALL BUST?
Built-in shape adds
fullness. *confidentially*

AVERAGE BUST?
Circular stitching creates
a softer, lovelier line

NEEDING UPLIFT?
Pre-formed cups give, and
keep, *that youthful line*

Silhouette HIDDEN TREASURE

Silhouette MERRY-GO-ROUND

Silhouette INNER CIRCLE

Secretly...comfortably...the HIDDEN TREASURE bra gives you the fuller, shapelier contours you long for...a beautifully rounded Silhouette — *without puffs*. HIDDEN TREASURE improves on nature *naturally*. The shape's built in — and never changes, never washes out. White Nylon. **29/6**. Longline Model, **42/-**. Strapless Model, **39/6**.
A cup 32″, 34″, 36″.
B cup 32″, 34″, 36″, 38″.

Net-lined, 4 section, circular stitched cups support...separate...shape your bust into soft, feminine contours. A 'can't-curl' band hugs you snugly at the diaphragm, ensuring complete, all-day comfort : your MERRY-GO-ROUND bra *can't* wrinkle or ride up. White Nylon.
B cup 32″, 34″, 36″, 38″, **19/6**.
Plunge-line, Nylon Voile, A cup 32″, 34″, 36″, B cup 32″, 34″, 36″, 38″, **19/6**.
Longline, B cup 32″—43″, **28/11**.

The bra of the age — for the line of youth. Pre-contoured cups lift years off your bust, bringing back the lovely line you thought you'd lost for ever. And because INNER CIRCLE cups are *permanently* curved, they keep their shape — and yours — through countless washings and wearings. White Nylon. A cup 32″, 34″, 36″, B cup 32″, 34″, 36″, 38″. **29/6**. Longline Model, B cup 32″, 34″, 36″, 38″, C cup 34″, 36″, 38″, 40″, **45/-**. Longline Strapless, B cup 32″, 34″, 36″, 38″, **49/6**.

Now - make your bust line your beauty line

49

film styling was not only thriving but was slowly seeping upwards from the bottom to the top. Worse, it was infiltrating culture too, as the new movement of 'pop art' celebrated American style and consumerism rather than condemning it.

By the end of the decade the idea of 'good design' itself was starting to look old-fashioned in comparison with the vivid style emanating from America. Now the consumer was in charge, not the designer, as the critic Rayner Banham declared in 1960:

> The concept of good design as a form of aesthetic charity done on the labouring poor from a great height is incompatible with democracy as I see it.

No plate of food was ever allowed to stand alone; there was always plenty on the table.

STEAK AND PASTRY RING *(Page 16)*

STUFFED BREASTS OF LAMB *(Page 15)*

SMOKED HADDOCK AND EGG SAVOURY *(Page 18)*

FRANKFURTER ROLLS IN PARSNIP CHEESE *(Page 15)*

We need, instead, a concept of good design as the radical solution to the problem of satisfying consumer needs.

This did not mean the end of the reign of the designer. Indeed, many of them had anticipated this shift: instead of lecturing the public directly on the importance of good design, they began to work with the manufacturers to provide good designs for consumers to choose. Ideas about what is now called 'brand image' but was then known as 'house style' became increasingly important, and many established designers set up as consultancies in order to provide this. Misha Black, whose designs had shaped the South Bank, had led the way with the founding of the Design Research Unit at the end of the war, but many other designers, like F. H. K. Henrion, Beverley Pick and Hans Schleger, were working in this way as the 1950s came to a close.

Although the most obvious applications of the idea were in retail and manufacturing, where a house style would communicate the company to the consumer, it spread to some quite surprising places – the Design Research Unit even created a uniform style for Watney pubs. Looking modern had now spread from the home into the whole consumer culture, and if a company wanted to make money, this seemed to be the only way to go.

The 'good design' of the Festival of Britain might have been going out of fashion, but the idea of being modern was not. In fact the complete opposite was true: the prophets of the 1950s had been so successful that the public was ready for an even newer style to match the new decade of the 1960s.

Food in the 1950s was always portrayed as abundant, in this case apparently dropping from heaven.

As the decade went on, not even pubs could escape the standardising attention of designers.

A NEW KIND OF
MODERN

<A NEW KIND OF MODERN>

A T THE END of the 1950s, Britain was a very different country from that of ten years previously. While some of this was due to social developments like the arrival of teenagers, television advertising and hire purchase, the biggest single change was in better standards of living. Thanks to the post-war rebuilding programme, many more people now lived in modern houses. Wages had doubled over the decade and with more money had come a whole range of affordable household goods, including fridges, stoves and even the first tumble dryers and dishwashers – along with, of course, the television. The technological age that the Festival of Britain had promised was now here to be lived in, and increasing affluence meant that more and more people were able to enjoy its delights. By the end of 1959, *Queen* magazine was describing this as 'the time of BOOM' and urging its readers to enjoy it.

The contemporary style ran through this consumerist paradise like the letters through a stick of rock. The splayed legs and contrasting colours, the pale woods and boxy furniture were now so ubiquitous that they had become a cliché. It was no surprise, then, that as the decade came to an end, people started to look for something new.

By 1960, many more houses had been improved by the new labour-saving appliances.

ours is a nice house, ours is

and in all the nicest houses from Hong Kong to Rio, from London to Sydney, you'll see Creda electric cookers, water heaters, kettles, irons and electric fires helping round the house.
Creda is also taming the World over for its exclusive range of Heavy Duty Cooking Equipment, which includes Unity' Restaurant and Chef Ranges, Grillers, Steamers, Boiling Table Hot Cupboards, etc.
Creda is part of the House of Simplex, famous for industrial products too : low-tension switch and fuse gear, flameproof equipment, conduit and conduit fittings, lighting equipment, Lundberg accessories, etc.
The cooker? That's the new Creda Comet—the last word in electric cookery

Creda and **Simplex**
products from one House

Simplex Electric Company Ltd. Oldbury Birmingham & Branches
A ⓣ COMPANY

Some of this was no more than fashion's need for novelty. Verticals were now emphasised, while oak and elm were being replaced by darker woods like teak and walnut. Patterns on fabric and wallpaper featured a broad brush and more painterly style rather than the scratchy Miro-esque lines that had characterised the start of the decade. But these changes were all linked: now modern design in Britain was looking more and more like International Modernism itself.

By the end of the decade, angular stylings and more muted colours were becoming popular.

The catalogues of companies like G Plan reflected this changing mood in design.

This 1959 design, Ducatoon by Lucienne Day, is far more painterly than her earlier textiles.

The times were right for this – if ever there was a moment to embrace the modern, the start of the 1960s was it. The country was poised between Macmillan's 'Never had it so good' affluence and Wilson's white-hot technological future. The energy and youthfulness that until now had been seen as American had started to spread to Britain too. People felt the need for a new style, and for one that was even more adventurous than anything that had come before.

This was able to happen because the contemporary style had not just run its course but done its work. At the start of the decade, it had been thought that the British would only ever be persuaded into the most gentle kinds of modern tastes, and even then very gradually. This was the rationale for contemporary design in the 1950s, but, much to everyone's surprise, the country had taken it to its heart. The doubters had been disproved, as the public preferred modern furniture over reproduction, abstract patterns rather than floral chintzes – less rather than more at last.

Her husband Robin Day's designs also became more sleek and rectilinear as the 1960s arrived.

Now, after nearly a decade of being softened up in this way, the British were ready for the real thing. Furniture was developing sleeker, simpler lines, while architectural designs jettisoned whimsy for glass walls and steel boxiness. In graphic design, the sans serif typefaces so beloved of the Europeans were starting to replace the Festival Egyptian and its offspring, while pottery and fabrics turned their back on hand painting and representation for more grown-up geometric patterns. Thirty years after the Stockholm Exhibition, Britain was embracing the ethos of the Modern Movement in popular design, with the result that the 1960s was going to have its own, very distinctive modern style. None of this would have happened, however, without the 1950s Modern which had led the way.

PLACES TO VISIT

Design Museum, Shad Thames, London SE1 2YD.
    Telephone: 020 7403 6933. Website: www.designmuseum.org
Geffrye Museum, Kingsland Road, London E2 8EA.
    Telephone: 020 7739 9893. Website: www.geffrye-museum.org.uk
Gordon Russell Museum, 15 Russell Square, Broadway, Worcestershire
    WR12 7AP.
    Telephone: 01386 854695. Website: www.gordonrussellmuseum.org
Victoria and Albert Museum, Cromwell Road, London SW7 2RL.
    Telephone: 020 7942 2000. Website: www.vam.ac.uk

FURTHER READING

Conekin, Becky. *The Autobiography of a Nation: The 1951 Festival of Britain*.
    Manchester University Press, 2003.
Ferry, Kathryn. *The 1950s Kitchen*. Shire Publications, 2011.
Hoskins, Lesley. *Fiftiestyle*. Middlesex University Press, 2004.
Jackson, Lesley. *Robin and Lucienne Day: Pioneers of Contemporary Design*.
    Mitchell Beazley, 2011.
Jackson, Lesley. '*Contemporary*'. Phaidon, 1998.
Kynaston, David. *Family Britain*. Bloomsbury, 2010.
Leighton, Sophie. *The 1950s Home*. Shire Publications, 2010.
Prichard, Sue. *V&A Pattern: The Fifties*. V&A Publishing, 2009.
Sandbrook, Dominic. *Never Had It So Good*. Little, Brown, 2005.
Turner, Barry. *Beacon for Change: How the 1951 Festival of Britain Shaped the
    Modern Age*. Aurum Press, 2011.

INDEX